The Human Body

The human body is made of organ systems. Each one has a job to do to keep the body working and healthy.

Cells

The human body is made entirely of fluids, cells and the products of cells.

Cells are the basic building blocks of life. Some are strong, such as the cells in bone, and some send electrical messages, like those in the brain.

Cells that have similar function are organised in groups and layers called tissues. Cells can reproduce, making the new cells needed for growth and replacement of damaged tissue.

Organs

Groups of tissues form organs, such as the skin, liver and heart. Organs are arranged into organ systems. For example, the stomach, liver and small intestine are organs of the digestive system.

There are organ systems for protecting the body from disease and getting rid of waste. Other organ systems allow the body to breathe, move and reproduce.

The organ systems work together, no matter what we are doing.

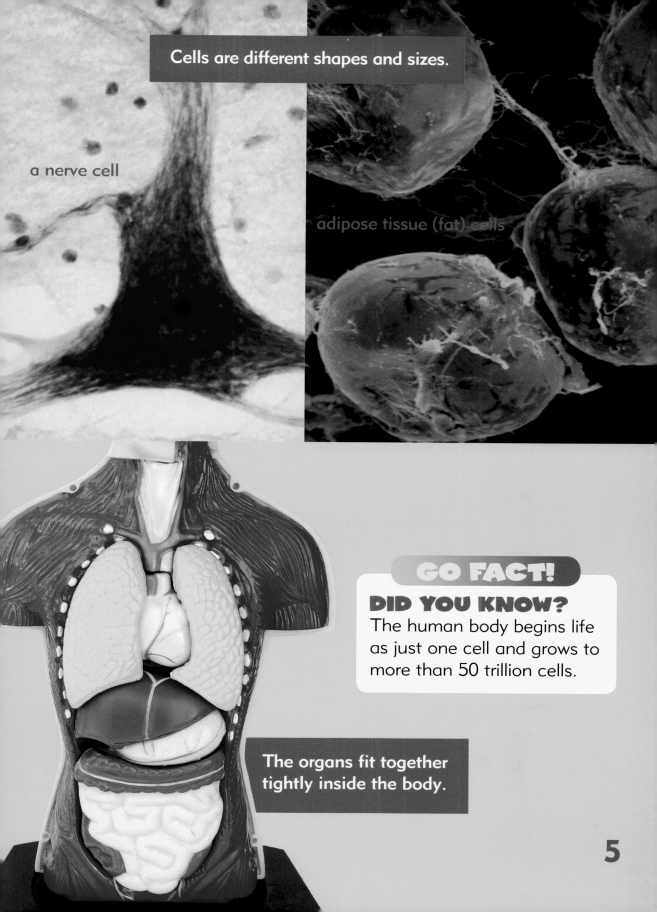

Cells are different shapes and sizes.

a nerve cell

adipose tissue (fat) cells

GO FACT!

DID YOU KNOW?

The human body begins life as just one cell and grows to more than 50 trillion cells.

The organs fit together tightly inside the body.

Bones and Muscle

The body is built on a **skeleton** of 206 bones. Muscles attached to the bones allow the body to move.

Bones

Bones support and protect soft tissues. The shape of a bone matches its function. For example, the bones in the head are flat and tightly joined to protect the brain. Holes running through bones carry blood vessels and nerves.

Bones store important **minerals**, such as calcium. The larger bones in the body contain **marrow**, where blood cells are made.

The longest bone in the body is the thigh bone, or femur. The smallest bones are the three in each inner ear.

Muscles

Muscles attached to the skeleton are called skeletal muscles. They work in pairs – one muscle to move the bone in one direction, and another to move it back the other way. Skeletal muscles are controlled by the nervous system.

When a skeletal muscle **contracts**, **molecules** inside the muscle's cells slide past each other. This is similar to the way your fingers slide past each other when you lock your hands together.

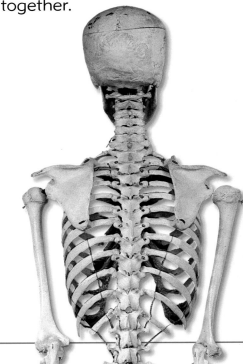

f they break, bones can heal. Sometimes a doctor puts screws through the bones to hold them together.

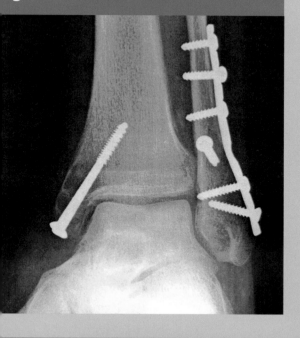

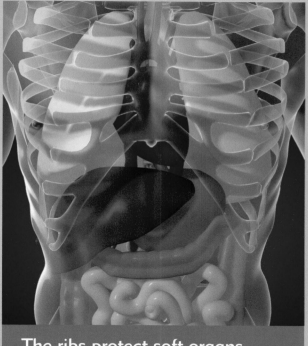

The ribs protect soft organs, such as the heart and lungs, underneath them.

Muscles work in pairs.

When this muscle contracts ...

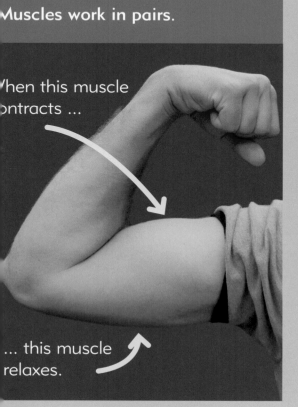

... this muscle relaxes.

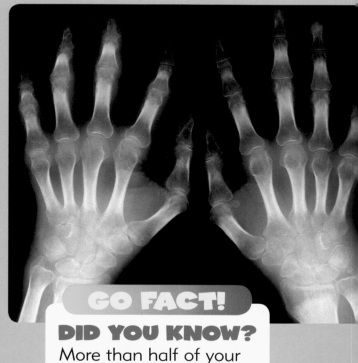

GO FACT!

DID YOU KNOW?
More than half of your bones are in your hands and feet.

7

Circulatory System

The circulatory system consists of the heart and blood vessels – arteries, veins and capillaries. It moves oxygen, fuel and waste around the body.

Blood

An adult has about five litres of blood. The heart pumps this amount of blood completely around the body in one to two minutes.

Blood is three to four times thicker than water. It consists of liquid, called plasma, and cells. Red blood cells carry oxygen from the lungs to all the cells of the body. White blood cells protect the body from disease by surrounding and destroying germs.

Blood vessels

The body contains more than 90 000 kilometres of blood vessels.

Arteries carry blood away from the heart. Veins carry blood back to the heart. Capillaries join the arteries and veins. They are the smallest blood vessels – most are thinner than a hair.

The body's two kidneys filter blood to remove waste. They also help the body control the amount of water in the blood.

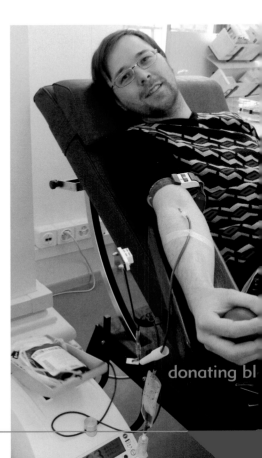

donating bl

Whose blood?

There are four main blood types: A, B, AB and O. Within these types, a person can be Rhesus Factor positive ('+') or Rhesus Factor negative ('–'). The Rhesus Factor type is written after the ABO type, eg A+, O–. A person can only receive some types of blood. What blood type are you?

Blood type	Percentage of UK population	A person with this blood type can receive type:
A	42	A and O
B	10	B and O
AB	4	A, B, AB and O
O	44	O

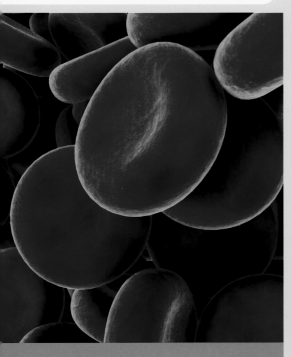

Red blood cells are redder when they are carrying oxygen.

The circulatory system looks like a road map of the body.

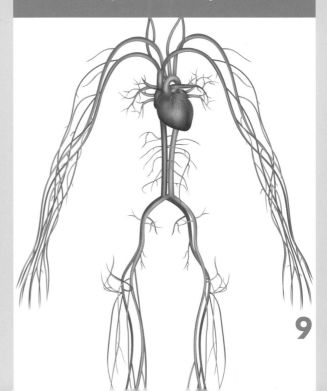

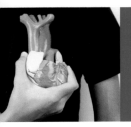

How Your Heart Work

The heart is a muscle. It beats about 35 million times per year. During an average lifetime, it wi pump enough blood to fill a supertanker.

The heart is the size of your fist and has four chambers. This is how blood flows through it.

1 Blood returning from the body enters the right atrium, which then contracts.

2 A valve opens to let blood into the right ventricle, which contracts and pumps blood to the lungs.

3 Blood full of oxygen returns from the lungs and enters the left atrium, which then contracts.

4 A valve opens to let blood into the left ventricle, which contracts and pumps oxygen-filled blood around the body.

The heart needs blood to work, just like any muscle – so it pumps blood to itself!

The heart's sounds are due to the heart vibrating as blood flows through it, and the opening and closing of its valves. A doctor uses a stethoscope at different spots on the chest to listen to the valves working.

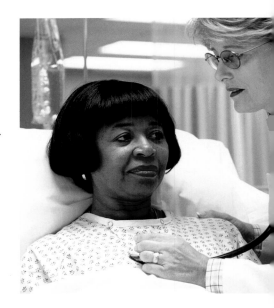

Schematic diagram of the heart

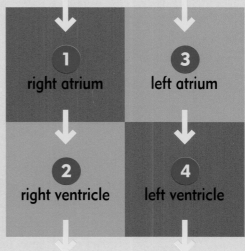

blood from body   blood from lungs

| 1 right atrium | 3 left atrium |
| 2 right ventricle | 4 left ventricle |

blood to lungs   blood to whole body

DID YOU KNOW?

A blood pressure reading measures the pressure of blood in the arteries. It is described as one number over another, such as '120 over 80'. The first number is the pressure when the ventricles contract. The second number is the pressure when the ventricles relax.

Model of the heart

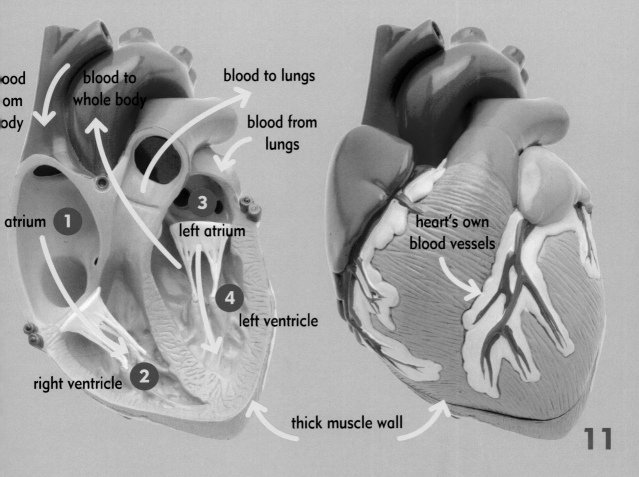

blood from body

blood to whole body

blood to lungs

blood from lungs

atrium 1

left atrium 3

left ventricle 4

right ventricle 2

heart's own blood vessels

thick muscle wall

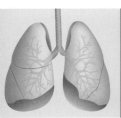

Respiratory System

The respiratory system brings oxygen into the body and removes carbon dioxide from it.

The body's cells need oxygen to survive, and carbon dioxide is one of their waste products.

Drawing breath

When you breathe in, muscles between the ribs and under the lungs contract. This pulls air into the nose. The space behind the nose, the nasal cavity, warms the air and makes it moist. It also filters out dust.

The air then moves down the trachea into the soft, spongy lungs. It flows through narrowe and narrower tubes in the lung At the end of the tubes are alveoli, which look like very sm balloons. There are about 300 million alveoli in each lung.

Exchanging gases

As the alveoli fill with air, oxyge passes from them into the blood vessels around them. At the same time, carbon dioxide passes from the blood vessels into the air in the alveoli.

When the muscles relax, the a and carbon dioxide is pushed out.

The lungs hold about six litres air, but only take in about half litre during quiet breathing.

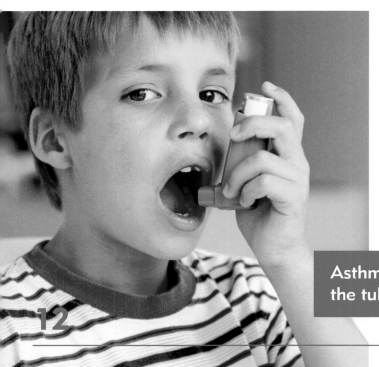

Asthma is a disease that makes the tubes in the lungs narrower.

sneeze rushes out the nose faster
an 150 kilometres per hour.

A peak flow meter measures how
much air can be forced out of the
lungs, and how quickly.

Smokers cannot hold as much air
n their lungs as nonsmokers.

THE LONGEST BREATH

In 2007, Tom Seitas held
his breath underwater for
9 minutes 8 seconds.

13

Nervous System

The nervous system controls what the body does and feels – the other organ systems cannot work without it.

Sending signals

The basic unit of the nervous system is the neuron. A neuron is a type of nerve cell. It sends and receives messages as impulses. An impulse is a tiny electrical charge that travels along the neuron at up to 360 kilometres per hour.

The nervous system also contains glial cells (*glia* means glue), which support and nourish neurons.

There are billions of neurons in the brain, spinal cord and **peripheral** nerves. Nerves are bundles of neurons. Neurons carry messages to and from the brain, and from one part of the brain to another. Sensory nerves carry messages from the surrounding world to the brain. Motor nerves control muscles.

Without you knowing

Many body functions, such as digestion and breathing, happen without the need to think about them. The nervous system controls them automatically.

A reflex is an automatic movement, such as blinking, that the brain does not control. A simple reflex is the knee-jerk reflex. Tapping below the knee cap with a small hammer stretches the thigh muscle. This causes the leg to kick forward. This reflex uses only two neurons – one that senses that the muscle has been stretched and one to make it contract.

testing knee-je reflex

14

ome nerves can regrow if they are
ut but many cannot, especially
hose in the spinal cord. This is a
lose-up image of neurons.

We blink every 3 – 5 seconds.

ram of a
or neuron

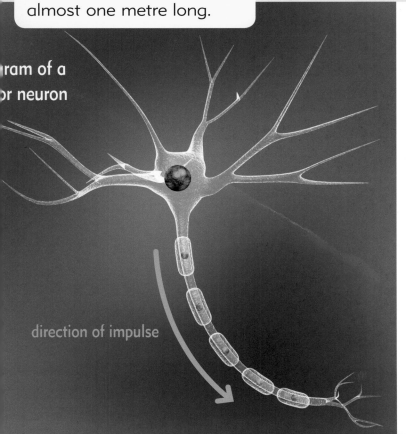

direction of impulse

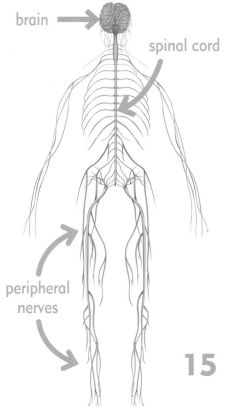

brain

spinal cord

peripheral nerves

15

The Brain

The brain contains about 100 billion neurons and one trillion glial cells.

Grey matter

The brain is soft and greyish pink, with a wrinkled surface like a walnut. The thin, outer layer is the most **complex** part of the brain. It produces thoughts, stores memories and controls language.

Both sides of the brain work together.

The brain is very delicate. It is surrounded by fluid and three **membranes**, which stop the brain from banging against the inside of the skull.

Two halves

The brain is divided into left and right **hemispheres**. The hemispheres are connected by millions of neurons, but they have slightly different roles in most people.

The left hemisphere is more concerned with how a person uses language – speaking, writing and reading.

The right hemisphere is more concerned with how a person understands shapes, colours, music, and their body's position and surroundings.

In every person, the left hemisphere controls skeletal muscles on the right side of the body, and the right hemisphere controls skeletal muscles on the left side of the body.

GO FACT!
DID YOU KNOW?

A 12 year-old's brain weighs about 1.3 kilograms – almost the same as an adult's brain

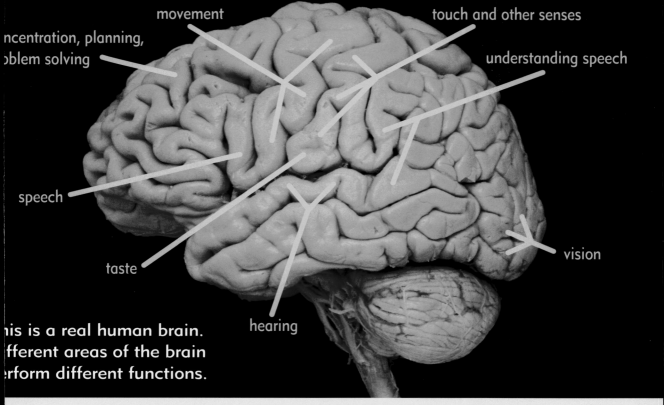

concentration, planning, problem solving

movement

touch and other senses

understanding speech

speech

taste

hearing

vision

This is a real human brain. Different areas of the brain perform different functions.

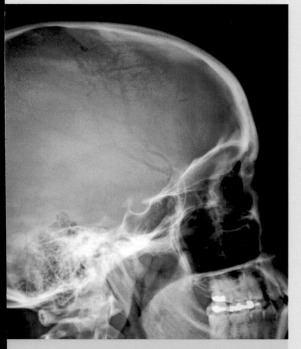

The skull consists of 22 bones, including 14 in the face and jaw.

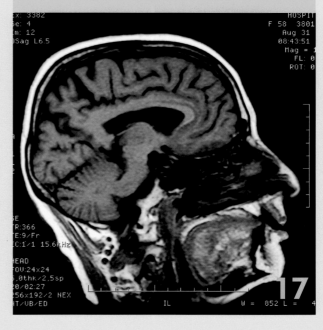

This scan of the head shows areas deep inside the brain that are important for emotions, learning and memory.

17

The Senses

The human body has five senses – vision, smell, touch, taste and hearing – that receive messages from the surrounding world.

Receptors

Each of our senses uses receptors. A receptor is a special cell or group of cells, and there are different receptors for the different senses. Receptors are **sensitive** to changes, such as changes in the amount of light or the squeeze from a handshake.

Nerves carry information from the receptors to the nervous system, which perceives the change and may respond to it.

Working together

Some receptors work together. Cold receptors in the skin are most sensitive to temperatures between 10 and 20 degrees Celsius. Heat receptors are most sensitive between 25 and 45 degrees Celsius. Below 10 degrees and above 45 degrees pain receptors let the body know that something is freezing or burning.

Many receptors adapt, which means that what the body senses fades over time.

An example is walking into a darkened room. It is difficult to see at first, but after several minutes the visual receptors adapt and allow you to see features of the room.

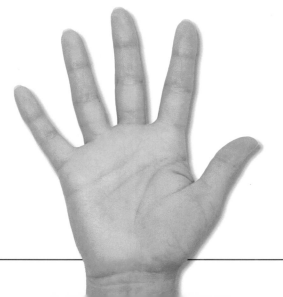

People are very good at remembering smells – maybe because the smell and memory areas of the brain are near each other.

Having two ears helps to detect where a sound is coming from.

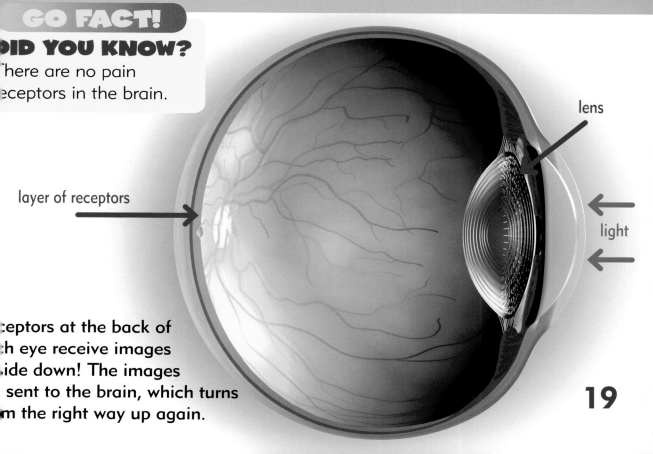

lens

layer of receptors

light

...ceptors at the back of ...h eye receive images ...ide down! The images ... sent to the brain, which turns ...m the right way up again.

19

Digestive System

The digestive system breaks food down into **nutrients** that the body absorbs. It expels whatever is left over.

A long path

Digestion starts in the mouth. Chewing breaks food into small pieces. Saliva contains an **enzyme**, which also helps to break food down. After swallowing, food moves down the oesophagus to the stomach.

The stomach uses acids, enzymes and its own moveme to turn the pieces of food into a thick liquid. It then squeeze: small amounts of the liquid in the small intestine, a twisting tube about six metres long.

The small intestine removes nutrients from the liquid and sends them to the liver. What is left over passes into the lar, intestine, which absorbs wate from it. The remaining waste, called faeces, is pushed out o the body.

The whole process takes 24– hours.

The body's factory

The liver acts as the body's factory and warehouse. It hel the body break down food, a then processes and stores it. also removes **toxins** and was from the blood.

stomach

liver

large intestine

small intestine

o help digestion, the best position r eating is sitting upright.

The growling sounds from your stomach and intestines are called borborygmus (say 'borba-rig-mus'). They are made as air bubbles move.

THE HOTTEST
The liver creates more heat that any other organ.

This is a close-up image of the nside of the small intestine.

Immune System

The immune system tries to destroy foreign bodies that attack the body.

The system consists of organs, **glands** and the cells they make. White blood cells are the most important part of the immune system. They **engulf** and kill foreign cells and **bacteria**.

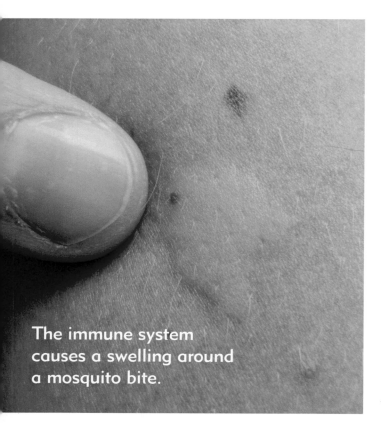

The immune system causes a swelling around a mosquito bite.

Getting protection

Vaccines build a person's **immunity**. A vaccine is a weak form of a disease, such as chickenpox. When a person receives a vaccine, the immune system makes cells to attack it. The person does not get sick because the disease is weak. Later, if the real disease strikes, the body has cells ready to attack and destroy it.

AIDS

AIDS is a disease caused by a **virus** that targets the immune system. AIDS stands for Acquired Immune Deficiency Syndrome. There are drugs to treat people with the virus, but a cure has not been found. If the immune system fails, the patient dies of an illness that the immune system would normally defeat.

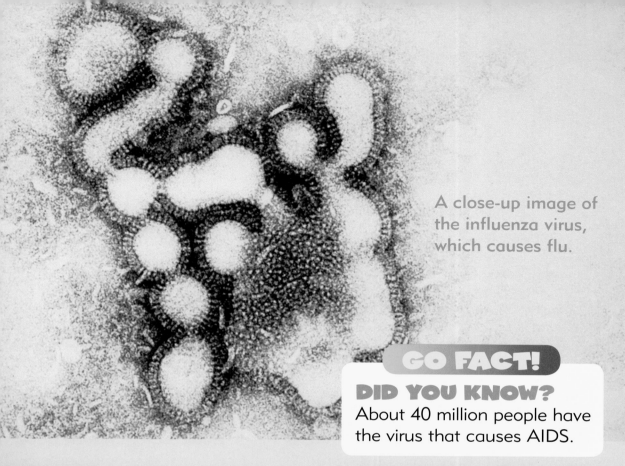

A close-up image of the influenza virus, which causes flu.

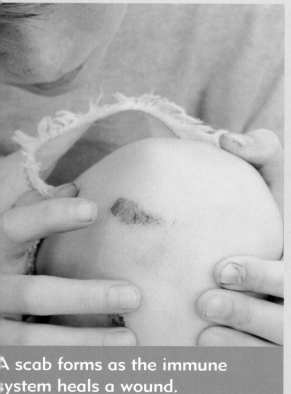

A scab forms as the immune system heals a wound.

Smallpox killed more than 300 million people in the twentieth century. But the smallpox vaccine eradicated the disease by 1977.

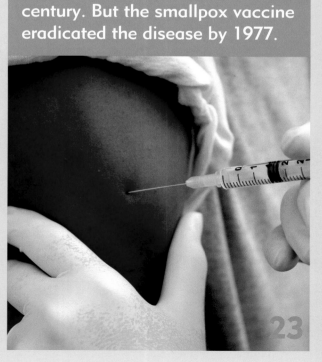

23

Reproductive Syster

The reproductive systems of males and female make different sex cells, which unite to make new life.

Source of cells

A female already has hundreds of thousands of sex cells, or egg cells, in her ovaries when she is born. A male makes sex cells, called sperm, in his testicles. Millions of sperm are made every day after he reaches **puberty**.

A new life begins when a sperm **fertilises** an egg cell. Sometimes two egg cells are fertilised by two sperm cells. This produces fraternal twins, who look no more alike than any other brothers or sisters from the same parents. If a single fertilised egg splits into two, identical twins grow – they are the same sex and very similar in appearance.

A place to grow

If fertilisation occurs, the new life grows inside the mother's uterus. The uterus, which is the size and shape of a small pear, is lined with thick, strong muscles. It grows 20 times heavier during pregnancy.

The mother feeds the growing baby through the **placenta**. Th umbilical cord joins the baby to the placenta. Nutrients and oxygen from the mother's bloo pass through the placenta into the baby's blood.

The baby is born after 40 week in the uterus.

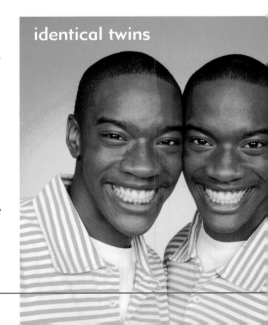

identical twins

he head of a sperm is 0.005 mm
ide. A sperm is 30 times smaller
an an egg cell.

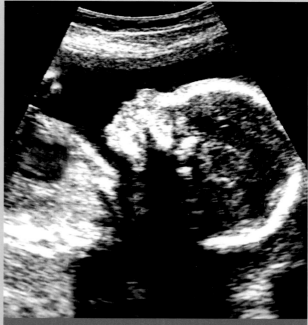

An ultrasound machine produces images of the baby inside the uterus.

THE MOST CHILDREN

A Russian woman in the 1700s gave birth to 69 children.

In the Uterus

You grow faster before you are born than at any other time in your life.

Time after fertilisation	Baby is about the size of a:	What is happening to the baby?
3 weeks	grain of rice	heart develops and starts beating
5 weeks	pea	body adds one million new cells every minute
8 weeks	large olive	all internal organs are present
13 weeks	peach	arms and legs start to move
26 weeks	small watermelon	eyes open and close

Endocrine System

The endocrine system helps to control almost every body function and organ. It affects mood, growth, how the body uses food, and the development and operation of the reproductive system.

Like the nervous system, the endocrine system sends messages around the body, but it uses hormones instead of neurons.

Hormones are chemicals **secreted** by organs and glands. Travelling through the blood, they act as signals from one organ system to another. In many cases, one hormone controls the release of other hormones.

Action stations

Adrenaline is a hormone made in the adrenal glands, which are on top of the kidneys. The glands release adrenaline when the body is shocked or in danger, helping it to be ready for action.

Adrenaline makes:

- the heart beat faster and stronger
- the liver release more sugar into the blood
- blood vessels widen
- airways in the lungs widen.

GO FACT!

THE TALLEST MAN

Robert Pershing Wadlow was 2·72 metres tall – almost twice the average height of a 11 year-old – when he died a the age of 22. Height is part controlled by growth hormon produced by a gland at the base of the brain.

A hormone causes a mother's breasts to produce milk for her baby.

Adrenaline makes the pupils **dilate**.

The pineal gland secretes the hormone melatonin, which helps to control the wake—sleep cycle.

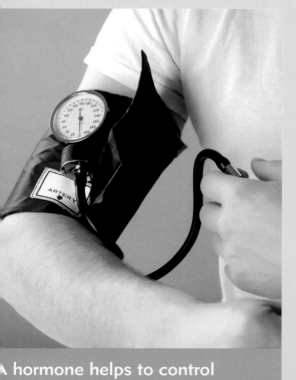

A hormone helps to control blood pressure.

27

Diabetes

Diabetes is a condition caused by too much glucose in the blood.

Using sugar

Glucose is a type of sugar and the body's main source of energy. The body uses insulin, a hormone, to convert glucose into energy. Normally, the pancreas, an organ just below the stomach, makes insulin. In diabetes, the pancreas doesn't do its job properly.

There are two types of diabetes.

Type 1

In people with Type 1 diabetes, the pancreas cannot make insulin. Someone with Type 1 diabetes must inject insulin into their body. They are very careful about what they eat and when. This helps control their glucose levels. A cure for Type 1 diabetes has not been found yet.

Type 2

People with Type 2 diabetes ca make insulin, but it doesn't wo as well as it should. As a result the pancreas makes more but never enough. Someone with this condition must stay active eat healthy food and not put o a lot of weight.

People with untreated Type 1 o Type 2 diabetes:

- feel thirsty
- are often tired
- are usually hungry
- pass more urine than usual
- may have blurred vision.

DID YOU KNOW?

Almost two million Britons may have diabetes. Many people don't know they have it.

People with diabetes test their blood often to find out how much glucose is in it.

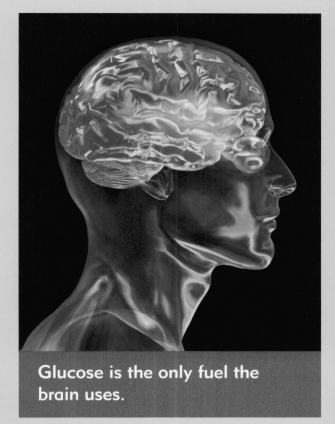

Glucose is the only fuel the brain uses.

INSULIN

People with Type 1 diabetes inject insulin up to four times each day.

The body turns some foods — such as hot chips, white bread and watermelon — into glucose faster than others.

10 Body Numbers

Sperm cells that try to fertilise one egg cell

400 000 000

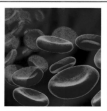

Days for a fingernail to grow one millimetre

10

Red blood cells in one millilitre of blood

5 000 000

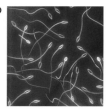

Muscles that move each thigh

9

Taste receptors on the tongue

10 000

Muscles that move each eyeball

6

Hairs that fall from the head every day

60

Litres of air that remain in the lungs at all times

1·2

Bones in the spine

26

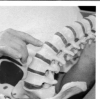

Sperm cells that can fertilise one egg cell

1

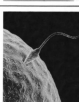

Glossary

bacteria (noun; plural of bacterium) very small organisms, which often cause disease

complex (adjective) involving many different parts, which makes it difficult to understand

contract (verb) to make or become shorter, narrower or generally smaller

dilate (verb) to become wider or further open

engulf (verb) to surround and cover completely

enzyme (noun) a chemical produced by cells; causes certain chemical reactions to happen in the body

fertilise (verb) to cause an egg to develop into a new life by joining with a male sex cell

gland (noun) an organ of the body that produces and releases hormones

hemisphere (noun; means 'half of a sphere') either half of the cerebrum, the largest part of the brain

immunity (noun) protection against a particular disease

marrow (noun) a soft, fatty tissue in the centre of a bone

membrane (noun) a thin layer of tissue that covers or connects parts of the body

mineral (noun) a chemical that the body needs to stay healthy

molecule (noun) the simplest form of a chemical

nutrient (noun) any substance that plants or animals use to get energy to grow

peripheral (adjective) at the edge or surface of something

placenta (noun) the temporary organ, formed inside the uterus, that feeds a baby inside its mother

puberty (noun) when the reproductive organs mature; it is usually ages 10–14 for girls and 13–16 for boys, although everyone is different

secrete (verb) to produce and release a substance, usually a liquid

sensitive (adjective) able to record small changes

skeleton (noun) the frame of bones supporting a body

toxin (noun) a poisonous substance, especially one produced by bacteria and which causes disease

virus (noun) a very small organism which causes disease

Index